A YOUNG VIC & THE OPERA GR(
CO-PRODUCTION

THE ENCHANTED PIG

Music by **Jonathan Dove**
Words by **Alasdair Middleton**

First performed at the Young Vic (1 December 2006–27 January 2007)

The Enchanted Pig tours to:

Northern Stage, Newcastle (31 January–3 February 2007)
Aldeburgh Music, Snape, Suffolk (10–11 February 2007)
Sheffield Lyceum (15–17 February 2007)
Richmond Theatre (27 February–3 March 2007)

Supported by

Commissioned with the generous support of the Peter Moores Foundation.
Licensed by agreement with Peters Edition Limited, London

THE ENCHANTED PIG

Music by **Jonathan Dove**
Words by **Alasdair Middleton**

King Hildebrand **John Rawnsley**

Mab, his eldest daughter **Kate Chapman**
Dot, his middle daughter **Akiya Henry**
Flora, his youngest daughter **Caryl Hughes** or **Anna Dennis**

The Book of Fate **Nuala Willis**

King of The East **Joshua Dallas**
King of The West **Delroy Atkinson**
The Pig **Rodney Clarke** or **Byron Watson**

Sun **Delroy Atkinson**
Day **Akiya Henry**
Mr Northwind **John Rawnsley**
Mrs Northwind **Nuala Willis**
The Moon **Joshua Dallas**

Old Woman **Nuala Willis**
Adelaide, her daughter **Kate Chapman**

Direction **John Fulljames**
Design **Dick Bird**
Lighting **Paul Anderson**
Movement **Philippe Giraudeau**
Musical Supervision **Stuart Stratford**
Music Direction **Ian Watson, Eddie Hessian**
Casting **Sarah Playfair**
Musical Theatre Casting **Anne McNulty, Sophie Hallett, Eleanor Lang**
Additional Casting **Pippa Ailion**
Costume Supervision **Caroline Hughes**
Assistant Director **Pia Furtado**

Stage Manager **Richard Llewelyn**
Deputy Stage Manager **Vicky Berry**
Assistant Stage Manager **Bella Lagnado**
Stage Management Work Placement **Kerry Sullivan**

BIOGRAPHIES

Delroy Atkinson
Sun / King of The West
Film includes: *Still Crazy* (Columbia Tri-Star); *Animal House* (Tiger Aspect/Sky). **Television** includes: *The Bill* (ITV); *Moon Monkeys* (BBC3); *From Bard to Verse* (Baby Cow/BBC). **Theatre** includes: *Poison* (Tricycle); *The Lion, The Witch and The Wardrobe* (West Yorkshire Playhouse); *Rent* (Prince of Wales); *Jerry Springer the Opera* (National Theatre/Cambridge Theatre); *The Bomb-itty of Errors* (New Ambassadors); *The Harder they Come* (Theatre Royal Stratford East); *Five Guys Named Moe* (National tour); *Twelfth Night, The Tempest, Our Country's Good* (Nuffield Theatre).

Kate Chapman *Mab / Adelaide*
Kate trained at the RSAMD (Cameron Mackintosh Scholarship) and with the National Youth Theatre. **Theatre** includes: *The Frog Princess, Far from the Madding Crowd, Once Upon a Time in New Jerzey* (RSAMD, The Fringe); *3 New Musicals* (Cardiff International Festival of Musical Theatre). **Concerts** include: *The Music of Hadjidakis* (Theatre Royal, Drury Lane); *West Side Story* (City of Oxford Orchestra); *An Evening of the Arts with HRH Prince Charles* (Holyrood Palace); *A Night at Gleneagles*; *NTY Yuletide Lunch* (Royal Garden Hotel, Kensington). **Cabaret** includes: *Funny Lass* (The Tron). **Television** includes: *Diastasi Christmas Special* (RIK1, Cyprus). **Recordings** include the *OCD Debut CD*, released in January '07 by Silverwood Music Group.

Rodney Clarke *The Pig*
Theatre includes: *Tobias and the Angel* (Young Vic). **Film** includes: *The Magic Flute* (Kenneth Branagh); *An*

After Image (BBC). **Opera** includes: *Don Giovanni* (Birmingham Opera Company); *Sante* (Aldeburgh); *Tangier Tattoo* (Glyndeboune Tour); *The Knot Garden* (Musical Theatre Wales); *Another America: Fire* (PUSH, Sadler's Wells); *Curlew River* (BBC3, Birmingham Opera Company); *The Marriage of Figaro* (English Touring Opear); *Iphigenie En Tauride* (Welsh National Opera). **Musical theatre** includes: *On the Town* (English National Opera). **Concerts** include: *Bernstein Mass* (London Symphony Orchestra). **Television** includes: *Flashmob – The Opera* (BBC2). **Voiceover** work includes: *World Rally Championships* (Channel 4).

Joshua Dallas
The Moon / King of The East
Theatre includes: *Once in a Lifetime* (National Theatre); *Reasons to Wake Up* (National Theatre Studio); *The Secret Garden* (RSC & West End); *A Streetcar Named Desire* (Clwyd Theatre Cymru); *The Boy Friend, The Pirates of Penzance* (Open Air Theatre Regents Park); *Sweeney Todd* (Bridewell Theatre). **Television** includes: *Ultimate Force Series 4* (ITV).

Anna Dennis *Flora*
Opera includes: *Ariadne, The Girl of Sand* (Almeida Theatre); *Orfeo* (English National Opera); *Ballo Delle Ingrate* (Birmingham Opera Company); *Siroe* (Oper de Zeit, Austria); *Rückert Lieder* (Streetwise Opera); *Cosi Fan Tutte* (Rosemary Branch Theatre). **Concerts** include: *Pierrot Lunaire* (City of London Festival); Mozart & Beethoven Masses (Clarion Society, New York); Shostakovich's Blok Lyrics (St John's, Smith Square); Berlioz &

Stravinsky Cycles (Britten Sinfonia); *Dido & Aeneas* (BBC Proms); *Alexander Balus* (London Handel Festival).

Akiya Henry *Dot / Day*

Theatre includes: *Coriolanus, Under the Black Flag* (Globe); *Coram Boy, Love's Labours Lost, Anything Goes* (National Theatre); *Ain't Misbehavin* (Sheffield Crucible); *A Midsummer Night's Dream, Just So* (Chichester Festival Theatre); *Skellig* (Young Vic). **Radio** includes: *Frankies Ballad* (BBC). **Television** includes: *Casualty, Doctors* (BBC). **Film** includes: *Calcium Kid, The Best Friend* (Working Title Films); *De Lovely* (Winkler Films).

Caryl Hughes *Flora*

Opera includes: *Red Riding Hood* (ENO Baylis: The Knack); *The Magic Flute, A Night at the Chinese Opera, Rinaldo* (Royal Academy Opera); *Cosi Fan Tutte, Le Nozze di Figaro, Der Stein Der Weisen* (Garsington Opera). **Television** includes: *Rownd a Rownd* (S4C); *Sinderela* (S4C/WNO). **Concerts** include: Welsh Singers Competition - Finalist (St David's Hall); Morriston Orpheus Choir - Winner (Brangwyn Hall); W.Towyn Roberts Award - Winner (National Eisteddfod of Wales); Teresa Berganza Masterclass (Purcell Room).

John Rawnsley
King Hildebrand / Mr Northwind

Theatre and **opera** includes: *Side by Side* by Sondheim (Opera Project); *Falstaff* (Stanley Hall Opera); *Stiffelio* (Holland Park Opera); *Doctor Dolittle* (Apollo Hammersmith & National Tour); *Charlie & The Chocolate Factory* (National Theatre Studio); *Cats* (New London Theatre); *Il Barbiere di Siviglia* (Glyndebourne); *Laura* (Watermill Theatre, Newbury);

Rigoletto (ENO); *Pagliacci* (La Scala, Milan); *Lucia di Lammermoor* (Royal Opera House). **Television** includes: *The Governor* and *The Bill*.

Byron Watson *The Pig*

Opera includes: *Tosca* (English Touring Opera); *Madama Butterfly* (Clonter Opera); *Le nozze di Figaro* (Edinburgh Festival Theatre); *Alcina, L'heure Espagnole, A Midsummer Night's Dream* (RSAMD); Glyndebourne Festival Opera Chorus. **Film** includes: *Tomorrow la Scala* (BBC Films). **Concerts** include performances for Channel 10, ABC, Radio 2GB and 2CH in Australia. Byron was a soloist with Northern Sinfonia, RSNO, Glasgow Symphony Orchestra and Buxton Symphony Orchestra.

Nuala Willis *Old Woman / The Book of Fate / Mrs Northwind*

Theatre includes: *Medea* (Almeida Theatre); *Sunday in the Park with George* (National Theatre). **Film and television** includes: *The Death of Klinghoffer, When She Died* (Channel 4). **Opera** includes: *Flight, The Second Mrs Kong* (Glyndebourne); *Eugene Onegin, A Midsummer Night's Dream* (Covent Garden); *The Rise and Fall of the City of Mahagonny* (Lausanne Opera); *Boris Godunov* (Zurich Opera); *Ballo in Maschera* (Canadian Opera); *Falstaff, Candide* (City of Birmingham Touring Opera); *Broken Strings, Snatched by the Gods* (Amsterdam & Almeida Theatre); *Ion* (Strasbourg & Aldeburgh).

Jonathan Dove *Music*

Jonathan Dove has written twenty **operas** of different shapes and sizes, including the highly successful airport-comedy *Flight*, first produced at Glyndebourne in 1998 and subsequently performed in Holland,

Belgium, Germany, Australia and America. He has written two operas for television and several chamber operas. An unusual achievement has been a series of 'community operas' in different parts of the country, sometimes involving several hundred performers in a single event. One of these, *Tobias and the Angel*, re-opened the Young Vic this year. **Other collaborations with Alasdair Middleton** include: *The Hackney Chronicles, Red Riding Hood, On Spital Fields* and the forthcoming *The Adventures of Pinocchio*. Jonathan has written the music for 30 **theatre** productions, most recently *His Dark Materials* for the National Theatre. From 2001–2006 he was Artistic Director of the Spitalfields Festival. In 1998 he was joint winner of the Christopher Whelen Award for his work in the fields of theatre music and opera. He is Music Adviser to the Almeida Theatre and is an Associate of the National Theatre.

Alasdair Middleton *Words*

Alasdair Middleton's work as a **librettist** includes *The World was all Before Them* and *On London Fields* (Winner of a Royal Philharmonic Award 2005) both for Matthew King, and *The Hackney Chronicles* and *On Spital Fields* (Winner of a Royal Philharmonic Award 2006) both for Jonathan Dove.

John Fulljames *Direction*

John is Artistic Director of The Opera Group. Previously for the Young Vic John directed the opening production in the new theatre, *Tobias and the Angel*. **Future and current productions:** *The Marriage of Figaro* (GSMD); *The Shops* by Edward Rushton (The Opera Group, UK Tour and Bregenz Festival); *Romeo and Juliet* (Opera North); *The Snow Maiden* by Rimsky

Korsakov (Wexford Festival). **Previous productions** include: for Opera North, *Saul* and *Hansel and Gretel* in semi-staged productions, and the *Little Magic Flute; Susannah*, Wexford Festival Opera, won the Irish Times Best Opera Production Award 2005; *Gentle Giant* by Stephen McNeff, ROH Education 2006; *Blond Eckbert* by Judith Weir, *The Nose*, Shostakovitch, Linbury Theatre and Tour 2006; *The Birds* after Aristophanes by Ed Hughes, World Premiere 2005 City of London, Cheltenham and Buxton Festivals, all for The Opera Group. **Other recent work** includes: Opera Showcase, National Opera Studio, Queen Elizabeth Hall; Essential Scottish Opera, Scottish Opera Tour; *Trojan Trilogy – Birds, Barks, Bones* by Edward Rushton – World Premiere, The Opera Group/ROH/Cheltenham Festival; *Bake for One Hour* by David Knotts – World Premiere, ENO; *Ariadne auf Naxos*, revival of production by Christof Loy, ROH; *Trouble in Tahiti/Mahagonny Songspiel*, The Opera Group, Buxton Festival 2004; *Girl of Sand*, World Premiere, Almeida Opera.
John's production of *Der Kaiser von Atlantis*, Opera Theatre Company, Dublin was the winner of Best Opera Production at the Irish Theatre Awards 2002.

Dick Bird *Design*

Theatre design credits include: *Harvest* and *Flesh Wound* (Royal Court), *Little Match Girl* (Tiger Lillies tour), *Chimps* (Liverpool Everyman and Playhouse), *Dirty Wonderland* (Brighton Festival for Frantic Assembly), *Lear* (Sheffield Crucible), *Tejas Verdes, Marathon* and *Une Tempete* (Gate Theatre), *The Night Season, A Prayer for Owen Meany* and *The Walls* (National Theatre), *Defence of the Realm*

(Peacock Theatre, Dublin), *The Wind in the Willows* and *The Lady in the Van* (West Yorkshire Playhouse), *True West* and *Great Expectations* (Bristol Old Vic), *Rabbit*, *Peepshow* and *Heavenly* (Frantic Assembly tours), *Those Eyes That Mouth* (Grid Iron, site specific at Edinburgh Festival), *Monkey!*, *The Three Musketeers* and *Poseidon* (Young Vic), *The Invisible College* (Salzberg Festival), *Light* (Theatre de Complicite tour and Almeida Theatre), *Closer* (Teatro Broadway, Buenos Aires), *Icarus Falling*, *Poseidon*, *The Invisible College*, *Half Machine*, and *Vagabondage* (Primitive Science) and *The Banquet* (Protein Dance UK tour). **Opera** credits include: *Un Segreto d'Importanza* (Teatro Communale di Bologna), *The Gondoliers* (Oper Am Rhein), *The Gambler* (Opera Zuid, Maastricht), *La Boheme* (English Touring Opera), *Die Kunst des Hungerns* (Schauspielhaus, Graz), *La Cenerentola* (Opera Theatre Company, Dublin), *Thwaite* (Almeida Opera), *Messalina* (Battignano Opera Festival), *Il Tabarro* and *Vollo di Notte* (Long Beach Opera Company), *Little Green Swallow* and *The Rape of Lucretia* (Guildhall School of Music and Drama), *La Boheme* (LVSO, Vilnius). He recently designed *The Canterville Ghost* for English National Ballet.

Paul Anderson *Lighting*

Paul Anderson trained at Mountview Theatre School and York College of Arts and Technology. **Lighting design** includes: *Julius Caesar* and *The Tempest* (current RSC productions); *Bent*, *On The Third Day*, *Someone Who'll Watch Over Me* (West End); *On Tour*, *Random and Incomplete Acts of Kindness* (Royal Court); *Turn of the Screw* (Bristol Old Vic); *Simply Heavenly* (Young Vic and West End); *A Minute Too Late*, *Stuff Happens*, *A Funny Thing Happened on the Way to the Forum*, *Measure for Measure*, *Cyrano de Bergerac*, *The Birds* (National Theatre); *The Resistible Rise of Arturo Ui* (National Actors Theatre New York with Al Pacino); *Lenny Henry's So Much Things to Say* (West End and international tour); *A Servant to Two Masters* (Royal Shakespeare Company and West End); *Twelfth Night* (400th anniversary production for Shakespeare's Globe at Middle Temple Hall); *Singer*, *Americans*, *The Inland Sea* (Oxford Stage Company); *Two Cities*, *Playing for Time*, *Taming of the Shrew* (Salisbury Playhouse); *20,000 Leagues Under the Sea*, *Shoot to Win*, *Pinocchio*, *Sleeping Beauty*, *Red Riding Hood*, *Aladdin* and *Cinderella* (Theatre Royal Stratford East); *Strange Poetry* (with the LA Philharmonic); *The Elephant Vanishes*, *Light*, *The Noise of Time*, *Mnemonic* (Drama Desk and Lucille Lortell award); *The Chairs*, nominated for Tony, Drama Desk and Olivier awards (Theatre de Complicite); *Knight of the Burning Pestle*, *Simply Heavenly*, *Arabian Nights*, *As I lay Dying*, *Twelfth Night*, *Guys and Dolls* and *West Side Story* (Young Vic Theatre); *Some Girls are Bigger Than Others*, *Pinnochio*, *The Threesome*, and *Lyric Nights* (Lyric Hammersmith); *The Christie Brown Exhibition* (Fragments of Narrative at the Wapping Hydraulic Power Station); *Rediscovering Pompeii* at the Academia Italiana (IBM Exhibition). **Fashion shows** for Fashion East, Lancome, ghd, Basso & Brooke, and AI international.

Philippe Giraudeau *Movement*

Studied dance in his home town of La Rochelle and worked as a professional dancer in France before joining London Contemporary Dance Theatre and Second Stride. In 1988 Philippe won the London Dance and Performance Award. He has worked in England as an actor: *Skriker* and *Pericles* (National Theatre), *Cherubin* (Royal Opera), *Le Bourgeois Gentilhomme* (Orange Tree), *A Mouthful of Birds* (Royal court), *The Princess of Cleves Secret Garden* and *IQ of 4* (ICA). As a **choreographer**, his work in opera includes: with director Tim Albery, *A Midsummer Night's Dream*, *The Merry Widow*; for The Metropolitan Opera New York, Janacek's *From the House of the Dead* for English National Opera. He collaborated with Robert Carsen on *Semele* and *The Cunning Little Vixen*, *Katya Kabanova* at the Vlaamse Opera, *Les Contes d'Hoffman*, *Alcina and Rusalka* at the Paris Opera, *Dialogues des Carmelites* for Netherlands Opera and La Scala, *Rosenkavalier* in Salzburg, *Traviata* for La Fenice, *Elektra* in Tokyo, *Manon Lescaut* in Vienna, *Iphigenie en Tauride* at the Lyric Opera, Chicago. Choreographed *Jenufa* in Amsterdam and *Chicago* for Richard Jones as well as *Pelleas et Melisande* for Opera North and ENO, *Juliette ou la cle des songes* at the opera Garnier, *The Trojans* at the ENO, and most recently *The Cunning Little Vixen* at the Nederland opera. With Antony McDonald, Philippe worked on *Aida*, *Samson and Dalila*, and *Snatched* by the Gods/Broken Strings for Scottish Opera, *Bernstein Wonderful Town* for Grange Park Opera. Collaborated with Stephen Langridge on *Arianna in Creta* for the Reis Opera and *Tangier Tatoo* for Glyndebourne Touring. For the Bregenzer Festspiele, *Un Ballo in Maschera* and *La Boheme*, both directed by Richard Jones and Antony McDonald. *Trovatore* directed by Robert Carsen.

Stuart Stratford
Musical Supervision

Born in Preston, Stuart Stratford read music at Trinity College, Cambridge, studying conducting with David Parry and at the St. Petersburg Conservatoire. Stuart is delighted to be working on Jonathan Dove's *The Enchanted Pig*, having also conducted his *Tobias and the Angel* and *L'altra Euridice*, and having been nominated for a Philharmonic Society award for his work as music director on *Palace in the Sky*. Highlights from his many **opera** credits include: the Calixto Bieito production of *Don Giovanni* at English National Opera; *Pagliacci* at Sadler's Wells for Opera North; *La Boheme* at the Royal Albert Hall; *Candide* with Birmingham Opera Company. Future plans: *Jenufa* at Opera Holland Park, *A Midsummer Night's Dream* for Opera North; concerts with the Manchester Camerata, the London Philharmonic Orchestra and the City of London Sinfonia.

Ian Watson *Musical Direction*

Ian graduated from the Royal Academy of Music in 2000 with the Dip.RAM, their highest performance accolade. He has a busy freelance career which has included performances with the CBSO, BSO, BCMG, London Sinfonietta, ENO, ETO, BBC NOW, BBC CO and BBC SO. He performs in 'The Czardas Duo' with 'cellist Matthew Forbes and together they have performed at festivals in the UK and Europe giving many premieres of new works written for them. Ian also appears with contemporary music ensembles *Icebreaker* and *Apartment House* and in summer 2004 joined the band of the *Divine Comedy* including appearances at Glastonbury and the Montreaux

Jazz Festival. He teaches at Kingston and Surrey Universities as well as Morley College and in July 2004 was Accordion and chamber music tutor at Dartington International Summer School. He has also adjudicated at festivals in the UK and Ireland. In May 2003 Ian became one of the youngest ever musicians to be honoured as an Associate of the Royal Academy of Music, an honour awarded to past students who have achieved distinction in the profession.

Eddie Hessian *Musical Direction*

Edward Hession studied accordion privately with John Leslie and piano at The Royal College of Music. His accordion can be heard on various film and TV soundtracks, including *Gosford Park*, *Captain Corelli's Mandolin* and *Shrek*. **Theatre** work includes London productions of *La Cage aux Folles*, *Les Miserables* (on keyboard), *Oliver*, *Theatre of Blood* and *Evita*. He has played with all the leading London orchestras, as well as the Royal Opera and ENO. He has worked with a wide range of artists, including Pavarotti, Westlife, Ronan Keating and Chris Rea. He performs with the gipsy-tango quintet called ZUM.

Sarah Playfair *Casting*

Sarah Playfair is a casting director working mainly in opera. Her career started with a secondment to Prospect Theatre Company and has included positions with London Contemporary Dance Theatre, ENO, WNO, Scottish Opera and ultimately Director of Artistic Administration for the Glyndebourne Festival and Administrator of Glyndebourne Touring Opera. Since 1998 she has been freelance, with regular clients Birmingham Opera Company,

Garsington Opera and Tête-à-Tête. Project work includes the Bethlehem Millenium Festival, Welsh Singers' Competition, First China International Singing Competition, BBC TV (*Figaro Live* and two *Flasmob* operas), BBCSO (*Turandot* and *The Second Mrs Kong*), Tiger Aspect Productions (*When She Died* and *Man on the Moon*) and Kenneth Branagh's recent film of *The Magic Flute*, which premiered at the 2006 Venice Film Festival and is due for UK release in 2007. She has worked regularly with Jonathan Dove, and recent work includes *Tobias and the Angel*, which opened the newly rebuilt Young Vic in October 2006.

Pia Furtado *Assistant Director*

Training includes The King's Head Theatre's Trainee Director's Scheme 2004, National Theatre Director's Course 2005, and Director's Placement at the Young Vic 2006, *The Enchanted Pig*. As an assistant director projects include *Flight 5065* at the London Eye (Royal Court@London Eye), *Bells* (Kali), *Hortensia and the Museum of Dreams* (Finborough) and *A Girl In A Car with a Man* (Royal Court). **Directing** credits include *Parade* (UK Premiere, Southside Edinburgh), *Our Miss Gibbs* (Finborough), *Leaving Home* (King's Head) and *All My Sons* (Bloomsbury Theatre). Pia has directed readings and workshops for companies and collectives including Burning Houses, Sourfeast, Kali and the Royal Court Young Writer's Programme.

THE YOUNG VIC

We are this country's leading home for younger theatre artists, especially directors. By presenting seasons of work by new directors in tandem with some of the great directors of the world – mingling youth and experience, ambition and genius – we hope to make the Young Vic one of the most exciting theatres in the world.

Many people, especially the young, believe that theatre belongs to 'others' of another class or another generation. But artists create for everyone. So we keep our prices low and, through an extensive program of Teaching, Participation and Research, we make a priority of finding and creating new audiences. 10% of our tickets are given away each year, irrespective of box-office pressure.

We believe a theatre should be a place of energy, intelligence and pleasure.

Join us in our new theatre whenever you can.

Young Vic
66 The Cut
London SE1 8LZ

www.youngvic.org
Tickets & information 020 7922 2922
Administration 020 7922 2800

The Young Vic is a company limited by guarantee, registered in England No. 1188209.
VAT registration No. 236 673 348
The Young Vic (registered charity number 268876) receives public funding from

THE YOUNG VIC

THE OPERA GROUP

The Opera Group is committed to creating innovative music theatre that enriches the lives of its audiences, artists and participants.

The Opera Group explores the full theatrical potential of music. The company's work is characterised by vibrant theatricality and vivid story-telling which comes to fruition in the moment of live performance. Two new productions are created each year, complemented by participatory, education and development activity that explores the future of the art-form and develops its potential relationship with existing and new audiences. In touring, the company seeks to work with national and international partners who share the company's desire to engage with the widest possible audience.

'It's incredibly rare to see ensemble work of this level in the theatre, let alone an opera with virtuoso singing included' *The Times*

'The Opera Group made the manic score sound like an established repertoire masterpiece.' *The Daily Telegraph*

'The Opera Group is a dynamic young company that brings great theatrical verve to the staid old world of opera' *The Guardian*

John Fulljames Artistic Director
Patrick Bailey Music Director
Sherry Neyhus Executive Producer

For further information or to support the company's work, please visit our website: www.theoperagroup.co.uk

The Opera Group is an Associate Company of The Young Vic Theatre

PETER MOORES FOUNDATION

The Foyle Foundation

The Columbia Foundation

THE SOURCE OF THE STORY

THE ORIGINS OF FAIRY STORIES are shrouded in myth and history. They emerge from an oral tradition of folk tales handed down over millennia. By their nature, folk tales are adaptable and acquisitive, incorporating elements from other stories and developing to suit their current audience. As a result it is often unclear whether similarities between stories point to a common ancestor or reflect shared cultural preoccupations and desires.

At certain moments in history, however, writers have collected and recorded the stories they have heard. This literary tradition provides a breadcrumb trail by which we may trace the development and tease out the interwoven strands of some of our most popular and enduring fairy stories.

The Young Vic's version of *The Enchanted Pig* derives from two literary sources: the first half is based on a Romanian folk story of the same name, and the second draws on a Norwegian folk story, *East of the Sun and West of the Moon*.

The first English version of *The Enchanted Pig* appeared in 1890 in Andrew Lang's anthology *The Red Fairy Book*. Lang had found the story in the German-language *Rumänische Märchen* (Romanian Fairy Tales) translated by Nite Kremnitz. Lang (1884-1912) edited twelve *Fairy Books* between 1889 and 1910.

Though a poet and novelist, his fairy books came out of his academic work as an anthropologist and historian and he stressed that he was the editor and not the original author of the tales: 'Who really invented the stories nobody knows; it is all so long ago, long before reading and writing were invented.' (Preface to *The Violet Fairy Book*, 1901)

East of the Sun and West of the Moon was first published in 1845 in a collection by Norwegian folklorists Peter Christen Asbjornsen and Jorgen Moe. It was published in English in 1849 in Anthony R Montalba's *Fairy Tales From All Nations*. In this version the animal bridegroom is a white bear, not a pig, but many elements of Alasdair Middleton's version (such as the character of the North Wind and the princess with an unusually large nose) are taken from this story. Novelist Angela Carter described *East of the Sun and West of the Moon* as one of the most beautiful and mysterious of the Northern European fairy tales.

Both stories belong to a tradition of fables about animal bridegrooms, the best known of which is *Beauty and the Beast*. *Beauty and the Beast* traces its written lineage to a second-century manuscript called *The Golden Ass*. In this tale, which contains a number of characters from Greek and Roman mythology, a young man is turned into a donkey by a witch, and a young woman is told the classical love story of Cupid and Psyche, in which Cupid falls in love with Psyche, who disobeys his order not to look at him, and must undergo a series of cruel trials at the hands of his jealous mother Venus before they can be united in love. Both story elements – the man enchanted in animal form, and the trials of star-crossed lovers – were interwoven in later adaptations such as *East of the Sun and West of the Moon*. The manuscript of *The Golden Ass* was uncovered in medieval Europe, became popular in the late Sixteenth and Seventeenth centuries, and versions of the story later appeared in many other published works. The story of Cupid and Psyche was translated from Latin into English by William Adlington in 1566, and the tale was commonly painted in the Fifteenth century on the trousseau chests of brides. John Milton refers to the story in his *Comus*, first performed in 1634 and published in 1637. It also reappeared as a play in seventeeth-century France, where it influenced stories created by Marie-Catherine D'Aulnoy, the celebrated fairy-tale writer of the French salons. D'Aulnoy also published a story called *The Green Serpent*, which contains reference to iron shoes, such as those worn by Flora in her journey across the universe.

The story of Cupid and Psyche was retold as *Beauty and the Beast* in 1740 in a novella by Madame Villeneuve. Another Frenchwoman, Madame Le Prince de Beaumont, published her own, considerably shorter version, in 1756. This latter version is the best-known and has been translated into other languages and retold by many other writers. The story was re-imagined from a feminist perspective by Angela Carter in The *Magic Toyshop* (1967) and by Disney as a film in 1991.

Another folk-tale tradition evident in *The Enchanted Pig* is that of the fatally curious woman. From Eve's consumption of forbidden fruit in the Judeo-Christian tradition and Pandora's catastrophic opening of the pro-hibited box in the classical tradition, stories abound of women seduced by curiosity to break the rules, who must then face the consequences. The most famous of these is probably *Blue-beard*, in which the heroine disobeys her husband and enters a forbidden chamber, only to discover the mu-tilated corpses of her predecessors. *Bluebeard* was already a popular folk tale when Charles Perrault published it in 1697.

The Enchanted Pig is a tale of witchcraft, disobedience, banishment, endurance, and the transformative power of love. Its many interwoven strands describe our most ancient and enduring dreams and fears, offering tantalising clues to who we once were, and what we might hope to become.

(Written by Kate Wild)

Alasdair Middleton
THE ENCHANTED PIG

OBERON BOOKS
LONDON

This edition of the libretto published by Oberon Books Ltd in 2006
521 Caledonian Road, London N7 9RH
Tel: 020 7607 3637 / Fax: 020 7607 3629
e-mail: info@oberonbooks.com
www.oberonbooks.com

The Enchanted Pig
A Musical Tale
Libretto © 2006 Alasdair Middleton
Music by Jonathan Dove © 2006 Hinrichsen Edition, Peters Edition
Limited, London

The right of Alasdair Middleton to be identified as the author of this
libretto of *The Enchanted Pig* has been asserted by him in accordance
with The Copyright Designs and Patents Act 1988.

Peters Edition Limited
Hinrichsen House
10-12 Baches Street
London N1 6DN
Tel: 020 7553 4000
Fax: 020 7490 4921
Email: copyright@editionpeters.com
www.editionpeters.com

The vocal score of *The Enchanted Pig* is available on sale from Peters
Edition Limited (EP 7785). The full conducting score and orchestral
parts are available on hire from Peters Edition Limited.

A catalogue record for this book is available from the British Library.

Cover illustration: CCF

ISBN: 1 84002 717 7 / 978-1-84002-717-4

Printed in Great Britain by Antony Rowe Ltd, Chippenham.

Characters

KING HILDEBRAND

MAB
his eldest daughter

DOT
his middle daughter

FLORA
his youngest daughter

THE BOOK OF FATE

THE KING OF THE WEST

THE KING OF THE EAST

PIG

AN OLD WOMAN

THE NORTH WIND

MRS NORTH WIND

THE MOON

THE SUN

DAY

THE MILKY WAY

ADELAIDE
daughter of the Old Woman

SOLDIERS

WILD GEESE

STARS

CLOUDS

SLAVES

CHORUS OF STORYTELLERS

Act One

A room in KING HILDEBRAND's palace. MAB, DOT and FLORA sewing.

MAB / DOT / FLORA: Destiny's needle is delicate
    And Destiny's thread is fine;
    I sit and embroider this pillowcase
    And wonder what man will be mine.

CHORUS: Look! Three princesses sit and wait.
    They wait for Love. They think Love's great.
    Love makes you the hero. Love makes you a fool.
    Love makes you happy. Love makes you cruel.
    Love is a long and blood-red thread.
    Love is a battlefield. Love is a bed.
    Love is a wonder, more strange than you'd think.
    It's a drug, it's the dregs of a poisonous drink.
    Love gives you blisters. Love leaves you blind.
    Love is the rarest jewel you can find.
    Till it's lost and you're left with a broken heart.
    Love is… Stop! It's time to start.
    Look! Three princesses sit and wait.
    They wait for Love.

MAB / DOT / FLORA: Destiny's pattern is intricate
    And Destiny's silk is strong;
    I sit and embroider this coverlet
    And wonder what takes him so long.

CHORUS OF SOLDIERS: (*Distant.*)
    Isn't war tremendous fun?
    You shake a sword,
    You fire a gun.
    Knock down a tower,
    Inflict some pain,
    Then you all come back again.

Enter KING HILDEBRAND, armed with his ARMY.

KING: Girls, d'you like my armour? Look! This bomb's brand
    new.
    Now. Why'm I here? Oh yes. I've come to say goodbye to you.
    I've just found out in Elfland there's a dam I haven't busted.
    I'm off to war. You're staying here. I know you can be trusted.
    Now girls don't think me negligent because I leave you
    here
    Alone and unattended – for one thing's crystal clear –
    A princess who is prudent can banish all her fears,
    If calmly, conscientiously, she to these rules adheres.

MAB / DOT / FLORA: Well, Daddy, we're all ears.

KING: Don't fall foul of fairies.

MAB / DOT / FLORA: We won't.

KING: Don't go kissing frogs.

MAB / DOT / FLORA: We don't.

KING: And don't you go mistaking
    Wolves for puppy dogs.
    If elves should do the housework
    It's only as a ploy,
    And always, girls, remember –
    A spindle's not a toy.
    Small old men with long grey beards
    Are always on the make.
    That gingerbread thing in the wood's
    A house and not a cake.
    Why don't you bet with pixies?

MAB: Because you can never win.

KING: That's right.
    A hag comes to the door with fruit?

DOT: We don't invite her in.

KING: How bright.
    If you go to a party
    Don't stay past the twelfth chime
    And mixing straw with spinning-wheels
    Leads to petty crime.
    Oh. There is one other tiny thing.

MAB / DOT: We don't doubt it.

KING: That small dark room at the end of the passage
    That no one goes into but me?

MAB / DOT: Well, what about it?

KING: Don't go in it or let anyone else in.
    Here, Flora, look after the key.

    He gives FLORA a key.

    She puts in her pocket.

    A distant fanfare.

    The bugle calls me. I must fly.
    Farewell, my daughters.

MAB / DOT: Bye then. Bye.

FLORA: If something watches over fathers
    Let that something hear this prayer.
    Keep my father and his armour
    Safely in that something's care.

MAB / DOT: So long, Daddy
    We'll be strong, Daddy
    Take as long, Daddy
    As you please.
    Better run, Daddy
    Here's your gun, Daddy
    We'll have fun Daddy
    With those keys.

KING: Now many's the monarch who'd think me stark mad.
    He has quite lost his head, they would say;
    When one thinks how young royalty goes to the bad
    When their mum or their dad's out the way.
    But my daughters are sensible, steadfast and strong.
    They are prudent and pretty and pure.
    So nothing could even begin to go wrong.
    Of that I am certain and sure.

CHORUS OF SOLDIERS: Isn't war tremendous fun?
    You shake a sword,
    You fire a gun.
    Knock down a tower,
    Inflict some pain,
    Then you all come back again.

Exit KING and ARMY.

FLORA: (*Looking out of the window.*)
    The army is embarking.
    The ships are on the sea.

MAB / DOT: The key, Flora.
    The key.

MAB: It's the moment we've been waiting for.

DOT: To find out what's behind that door.
    We'll just take a quick peek.

FLORA: I won't.

MAB: You freak!

FLORA: He left the key with me.

MAB: You're such a little goody-goody.

DOT: Daddy won't find out. How could he?

MAB: Unless you tell him.

FLORA: I won't.

MAB: Well then.

FLORA: He…

MAB: Just give it me, now!

FLORA: I won't.

MAB gets the key from FLORA.

Ow! Cow!

MAB: Come on! Hurry! Follow me!

*The three PRINCESSES run down a dark corridor towards
a forbidding door.*

MAB / DOT: What's behind the door, d'you think?
What d'you think we'll see?
What can be so wonderful
We're not allowed to see?

FLORA: I should stop them –
But I couldn't.
If I could stop them –
I wouldn't.

MAB / DOT: What's behind the door, d'you think?
What d'you think we'll see?
What can be so wonderful
It's under lock and key?

MAB: I bet it's something gorgeous.

DOT: Gorgeous! A lovely surprise! Sweets!

MAB: Wedding dresses! Perfume! Ocelots! Jewellery!
Fur Coats! Muffs! Stoles and stuff!

DOT: I think I need a wee.

FLORA: I know it's wrong –
    But it's exciting.
    Why's what's right
    So uninviting?

MAB: Of course, it could be something really gross.

DOT: Really gross! The shock of your life! Guts!

MAB: Loads of pickled reptiles in jars along a shelf –
    Peering at you – beady-eyed.

DOT: I'm going to wet myself.

FLORA: Why is right so unappealing?
    Why does wrong give you this feeling?

MAB: A really scary lunatic that froths and raves and rants.
    He grinds his teeth. He rolls his eyes.

DOT: That's it. I've wet my pants.

MAB: Maybe, hanging by their hair are all of Dad's ex-wives.

DOT: Now you're being silly.
    Daddy hasn't got any ex-wives.

MAB: That we know about.
    It's always the quiet ones that lead the double lives.

MAB / DOT / FLORA: What's he got locked up d'you think?
    Why the mystery?
    What can be so terrible
    We're not supposed to see?
    Open the door!

    They turn the key and enter a dark room, empty except for a large book on a plinth.

    Look!

DOT: (*Shielding her eyes.*)
    Look!

I can't look.
You look!
What is it?

MAB: It's a book.

DOT: A book?

FLORA: A book.

MAB: What a bore.

DOT: Just a book.

MAB: Just our luck.

DOT: What's it called?

MAB opens it and reads the title page.

BOOK: The Book of Fate.

FLORA: Let's get away – before it's too late.

BOOK: Read me. I'm the Book of Fate.
    Be it soon or be it late,
    If you read it, it will be;
    Leaf between my leaves and see.

FLORA: Come away. Come away.

BOOK: Be it soon or be it late
    If it's in the Book of Fate;
    What you read and what you see –
    Once you know it, it will be.

DOT: What, everything that's going to happen's written in
    that book?

MAB: Yes.

DOT: Well that's worth a look

MAB: Let's look and see.

FLORA: No. Don't.

MAB: Oooh look – here's me.

BOOK: Eldest Princess,
    Read me and see.
    The King of the West
    Your husband shall be.

DOT: Blimey.

MAB: It's just the sort of fate that I expected.
    Me, adored, obeyed, respected.
    People saying, 'Yes, Your Majesty.'
    People waiting, hand and foot on me.

DOT: Yes. But will it come true?

MAB: Bound to.

DOT: Queen of the West. Lucky you.

MAB: Now you.

FLORA: I don't think we ought to.

MAB: Oh come on.

DOT: It's just a bit of harmless fun.
    See, here's me!

BOOK: Middle Princess,
    Look here and see,
    The King of the East
    Your husband shall be.

DOT: Oh what a delicious fate,
    Like strawberries and cream,
    Like a kind of party
    An angel might throw in a dream.
    But it won't come true.

MAB: It's bound to.
   Queen of the East.
   Good for you.
   Now you.

FLORA: I don't want…

MAB: Well, you're going to.
   Look here's you.

BOOK: Youngest Princess,
   Listen to me
   A pig from the North
   Your husband shall be.

MAB: Oh.

FLORA: Oh no.
   A pig.

BOOK: From the North.

MAB: You're going to marry some thing that lives on a farm.

DOT: You must be devastated. Try to stay calm.

MAB: Not even a farm. More like a sty.

FLORA: A pig. But why?

DOT: It does seem a shame.
   It can't be right.
   Read it again.

BOOK: My words were quite simple.
   The letters were big.
   The youngest princess
   Shall marry a pig.

FLORA: The sun's gone black
   And the moon's turned red

And a cold wind blows
Round a dark pig's bed.

MAB: I wouldn't worry if I were you.
    Probably only a bit of it's true.

FLORA: Which bit?

MAB: The good bit. The bit about me.

FLORA: No. It's true.
    It will happen to me.
    It will happen to you.

CHORUS: (*Distant.*)
    That war was tremendous fun.
    We blew up towers.
    We fired the gun.
    We gave the enemy some stick.
    And who'd have thought we'd be so quick?

MAB / DOT: It's Daddy.
    He's back.
    Dry your eyes.
    Blow your nose
    And make sure
    He never knows.
    Close the door.
    Now lock it.
    Put the key
    In your pocket.
    It was just harmless fun.
    He's coming.
    Run.

In panic the GIRLS lock the door and hurtle down the corridor and run smack into…

End of Act One.

Act Two

A room in the palace. Enter KING HILDEBRAND and his ARMY with THE KING OF THE WEST and his friend, THE KING OF THE EAST, interestingly and romantically disguised.

ALL EXCEPT PRINCESSES: That war was tremendous fun.
    We blew up towers.
    We fired the gun.
    We gave the enemy some stick.
    And who'd have thought we'd be so quick?

KING: (*Kissing MAB and DOT.*)
    Hello, girls! I'm back. We won!

MAB / DOT: (*Breathlessly.*)
    Well done.

KING: Flora dear, I haven't kissed you,
    But you're crying.

FLORA: I…

MAB / DOT: She missed you.

FLORA: We…

DOT / MAB: She missed you very, very much.

KING: Did you dear I'm really touched.

FLORA: (*Handing her father back the key.*)
    The key.

KING: (*Pocketing it.*)
    Ah, yes the key.

FLORA: We…

MAB / DOT: (*Steering FLORA firmly away.*)
    Flora dear,

Come over here.
She cried so much, she's still quite weak.
You really oughtn't try to speak. (*They nip her.*)

FLORA: Ow.

MAB: (*Smiling at her Daddy.*)
But how did you get back so soon?

DOT: (*With exaggerated interest.*)
There's the mystery.

MAB: It must have been the quickest war in history.

KING: Good question, girls. You see this fellow here?

MAB: (*Bowled over by the beauty of THE KING OF THE WEST.*)
Do I?
His kingly brow, his eyes so blue and clear,
His nose where majesty and sweetness blend…

DOT: (*Bowled over by THE KING OF THE EAST.*)
Umm.
I prefer his friend.

KING: This fellow here was out with his army on manoeuvres
in a wood.
We marched to Elfland together. We beat them quickly.

KINGS OF WEST & EAST: (*Bowled over by the beauty of MAB
and DOT.*)
And we beat them good.

KING: His friend here of obscure but doubtless noble birth
Also played a part.

*MAB and DOT gaze longingly at THE KINGS OF THE WEST
& EAST.*

DOT: I think he's the most gorgeous man on earth.
He has my heart.

MAB: His medals.

DOT: His muscles.

MAB: His eyes so brown.

DOT: Look at his profile.

MAB: Look at his crown.

KING: But, girls, I haven't told you the best.
He's the King of the West.

ALL PRINCESSES: The King of the West!!!

During the following THE KING OF THE EAST and DOT slowly move apart and talk.

MAB never takes her eyes off THE KING OF THE WEST.

FLORA: Not the King of the South?

MAB: Flora, shut your mouth.

KING: And guess what I promised him for helping me out.

FLORA: Some toffee?

DOT: A third of your land?

KING: Do I look mad?

MAB: Well, Dad,
If I had been you I would have promised him
My beautiful eldest daughter's hand.

KING: Exactly.

KING OF WEST: Exactly.

MAB: Exactly.

KING OF WEST: Princess, if you marry me,
You will,

Of diamonds and tiaras never have your fill.
Will you?

ALL EXCEPT FLORA: Isn't love a beautiful thing?

MAB: And isn't this a beautiful ring.
Look, Flora, Rubies.

FLORA: (*Aside to MAB.*)
Don't you see?
It's coming true.
It came true for you.
It will come true for me.

MAB: Flora, dear, don't get so tense.
It's all just a coincidence.

KING OF EAST: (*Coming forward, hand in hand with DOT.*)
Oh King,
I'm only a humble nobleman,
But both of us think that it's meant –
I've asked your daughter to marry me
And we would like your consent.

DOT: He's only a humble nobleman
Daddy, he's not a king,
But, Daddy, I know I love him
And look at the size of this ring.

KING: It is not what I expected,
But true love should be respected,
Your proposal – I accept it.

ALL EXCEPT FLORA: Isn't Love a beautiful thing?

MAB: (*Aside to FLORA.*)
There! Where's the Book of Fate now?
She's married some random nobleman.
The silly cow.

KING OF EAST: Princess, King, I have a surprise.
All my life I have wanted to be loved just for myself,
Not for my titles, my land, or my wealth.
All this time I've been in disguise.
Actually, I'm the King of the East.

He flings off his disguise revealing a splendid uniform. He takes his crown from his pocket and puts it on.

ALL: He's the King of the East.

KING OF EAST: Princess if you marry me, you will
Go to expensive restaurants every night
And never have to pay the bill.
Will you?

DOT: I will.

FLORA: What am I going to do?
It's all coming true.

MAB / DOT: Stop making such a fuss.
Can't you just be happy for us?

FLORA: Everything's going so badly.

EVERYBODY ELSE: Everything's going so well.

KING OF EAST: But there's a terrible smell. What can it be?

DOT: A terrible smell –
Well, don't look at me.

KING OF WEST: And that noise.
A sort of snorting.

MAB: Grunting.

DOT: Squealing.

FLORA: I've got the most uneasy feeling.

DOT / MAB / KINGS: (*At the window.*)
>And look there!
>Pigs! Pigs everywhere!
>Boars and piglets! Porkers! Sows!

Knocking at the door.

KING: Something's banging at the door.
>A heavy hand.

MAB: More like a paw.

More knocking.

KING: Something's banging at the knocker.

MAB: Less like a paw,
>More like…

FLORA: A trotter.
>It's the Pig from the North.
>Find me somewhere to hide.

PIG: (*Outside.*)
>King! King! Let me inside.
>I have come for my bride.

KING: (*Peering through the keyhole.*)
>We have no brides for talking pigs here.
>Don't worry, Flora, you've nothing to fear.
>Open the door.

FLORA: (*Barring the door.*)
>No, don't let him in.

KING: Don't forget I am King.
>A king is a match for a pig any day.
>Get out of the way.

The doors open.

Enter PIG.

ALL: That pig is hairy.
    Kind of pinky.
    Rather scary.
    Very stinky.

PIG: Dragged by Fate's magnetic tide
    I have come to claim my bride.

KING: Now, Pig, let me make one thing clear,
    We have no brides for you here.

PIG: King, do you dare
    To meddle with Fate?
    My bride stands there.

He goes to FLORA.

KING: My daughter?
    What has she to do
    With you
    Or Fate?

PIG: The Book has been opened.
    The words have been read.
    Dragged from the North
    I have come to be wed.

KING: (*To FLORA.*)
    You opened the door that should stay locked?
    You read the Book of Fate?

MAB / DOT: She did.

FLORA: I did.

KING: Then it's too late.
    Once you've read it, it must be.

PIG: Princess, you must marry me.

He takes FLORA's hand.

Come on, wife! I can't wait.
You are mine it is your fate.

FLORA: Father, you're a king.
Kings make fate.
Father, do something.
It can't be too late.

PIG: Princess come, my sty awaits.

He pulls her to the door. Her crown falls off.

FLORA: Father, don't you love me?
Can you see me led
Uncrowned, to a pig's bed?

KING: You are as dear to me as life
But Fate is a fact,
Like the moon or the sun.
There is nothing to be done
But be his wife.

FLORA: Father!

KING: Fate is iron.
It can't be broken.
A king must be silent
Once Fate has spoken.

FLORA: Daddy!

KING: There is nothing I can do.

MAB / DOT: And the streets are full of poo.

KINGS OF WEST & EAST: Princess, marry the pig.
Yes, his farts are obscene
But I'm sure his sty's clean.

FLORA: Princesses do not marry pigs.
That's not the way life should be.

A pig desires a human bride.
But why did Fate pick me?

DOT / MAB: Princess, marry the pig.
Yes, he's a bit surly
But his tail's sweet and curly.
Princess, marry the pig.

FLORA: Ugly, dirty, smelly swine.
How can I scrub off this fate of mine?

MAB: Oh, just hurry up and be the pig's wife.
You're ruining what's supposed to be the happiest day
of my life.

KINGS OF WEST & EAST: Princess, marry the pig.
Yes, he snorts and snuffles
But he'll find you nice truffles.
Princess, marry the pig.

KING: Fate's laws are iron
That will not bend nor rust.

PIG: Princess when you marry me,
You will,
Live in a pigsty and dine upon swill.
Will you?

FLORA: I must.

MAB / DOT / KINGS OF EAST & WEST: Princess, marry
the pig.

PIG: Princess, come, my sty awaits.

MAB / DOT / KINGS OF EAST & WEST: Princess, marry
the pig.
Yes, his poo might stink
But he's your shade of pink.

KING: Maybe it isn't as bad as it seems,
    Two of my girls have the men of their dreams.
    Maybe – who knows? – after a while
    We'll look back on this and be able to smile.
    Maybe it's all for the best somehow.
    Maybe it isn't as bad as it seems…now.

End of Act Two.

Act Three

CHORUS: Let's get on with this wedding!
    Imagine the bells.
    Imagine the cake.
    Imagine the vows
    That the Princesses make.
    After the marriages
    Into the carriages.
    Imagine confetti.
    Imagine the cheers.
    Two leave in laughter.
    One leaves in tears.
    One to the sunset.
    One to the dawn.
    One to the North
    Forlorn.
    In the coach
    The Princess weeps,
    Pig sleeps,
    Pig snores,
    Dreams the dreams of happy boars.
    Roots, potatoes, piggy meals.
    The world turns to mud
    Beneath the coach's wheels.
    The Princess stares ahead at life.
    Pig's Wife.
    The carriage stops.
    Pig wakes.
    He lifts the Princess down.
    Takes a look around.
    Her white Princess's satin slippers sink into the muddy
        ground.
    It's cold, it's wet, it's dark, it's late.

North.
They stand before Pig's palace gate.

PIG: Now we're nearly home.
Look.
Mud.
A lovely pool of bubbly mud.
Churning, chestnut, chocolate pool;
Thick, relaxing, tempting, cool –
To quench the fires of swinish blood.
I must go in.
Now kiss me.
Now roll in the mud.
Now we're the same.
Now kiss me again.

FLORA: I've just thought, I don't know your name.

PIG: Pig. I am Pig.
Now we're home.

CHORUS: Pig's Palace.
Cleaner than you'd think.
Lots of marble.
Balustrades, torches.
Up the stairs
Princess's bedroom.
Gold and pink.
Ornate mirrors.
Miles of gilded wood.
Looks just like a princess's bedroom should.
The moon sits in an open window
His light on the floor
A pool of white.

FLORA: Mud.
Moon.
Mud.

I kissed a pig.
I rolled in the mud.
And somehow,
Somewhere,
It felt,
Well, not how I thought it would.
It felt,
In some way,
Good.
Moon,
What does it mean?

PIG at the door.

PIG: Princess, are you there?

FLORA: Yes, Pig, I'm here.

PIG: You do not sleep?

FLORA: No.

PIG: Or weep?

FLORA: Pig, I neither sleep nor weep.
    I wait.
    I wait for you.
    Come and sit.
    Let's talk a bit.

PIG: It's getting late.

FLORA: Pig, wait.
    Stay.
    You turn your head away.
    Why?

PIG: I don't know.
    I'm shy.

FLORA: Pig, do you cry?
  Why?

PIG: Your beauty makes me cry.

FLORA: Does beauty make pigs cry?
  Why?

PIG: It's so near.
  Your beauty is so close to me.
  It comforts me. It tortures me with what might be.

FLORA: Pig, come here.
  Let me dry your eyes.
  What beautiful eyes you have.
  Like pools, like jewels, so deep, so clear,
  And something,
  Oh!
  So sad, like hope or fear.
  How did I never see your beautiful eyes before?

PIG: There's something there in your eyes too.
  Can it be?

FLORA: What?
  What do you see?
  Tell me.

PIG: I can't say its name.

FLORA: Why?

PIG: I'll go back to the sty.

FLORA: No.
  Don't go away.
  I want you to stay.
  Pig!
  Husband!
  Stay!

PIG: Husband you call me?

FLORA: Husband I call you.

PIG: Then Husband I come!

PIG is transformed into a handsome prince.

FLORA: Ah! Look! You're a man!
A man! A king!
Isn't Fate a wonderful thing?
Arms open wide to embrace me.
I must go in.
Now we're the same.
I've just thought, I don't know your name.

PIG: Husband. I am Husband.
Now we're home.

CHORUS: Oh mystery! Oh wonder! Oh thing that can't be
told!
Oh pool of shining silver. Oh tower of burnished gold.
Fear has been forgotten. Difference is past.
A princess and a pig have met and found themselves at last.

FLORA: I was a princess,
I had a crown, a throne,
I had a father, two sisters,
And I was alone.

PIG: And I was a king,
I had a world of my own.
I was surrounded by people
And I was alone.

PIG / FLORA: But now I have you.
Someone to know me,
Someone to show me
How full life can be.

CHORUS: (*Distant.*)
> The moon is slipping off to rest,
> And something stirs in every nest.
> Birds stretch their wings to greet the dawn,
> Their beaks melodiously yawn.

PIG: (*Turning back into a pig.*)
> No. No. I must go.

FLORA: Go? Where?

PIG: Back to my sty.

FLORA: No. What's the matter? What's happening?

PIG: Get back. I'm changing back. I must go back.
> Soon it will be day. Soon I will be a pig again.

FLORA: No! Stay!

CHORUS: Night's candles are all burned out
> And soon his nose will be a snout.
> Pink and squinty piggy eyes
> See the sun climb up the skies.

PIG: Day.
> Pig again.
> I'll be a man
> When the sun has set.

FLORA: So the spell's not broken yet?

PIG: Not completely.
> If you want to free me,
> Just love me,
> Just trust me.
> Be patient.
> I will be free.

FLORA: There must be a quicker way. There must.

PIG: Love – Princess – Patience, Trust.

Exit PIG.

CHORUS: Princess, the sun is in the sky.
  And your husband's in the sty.
  But enjoy the warm sunlight
  He'll be a man again tonight.

One morning in the gardens of PIG's palace.

FLORA: Love. Patience. Trust.
  Pig! Husband!
  I love you.
  I trust you.
  I can be patient.
  But I want to free you.
  There must be something I can do.
  There must.
  Something quicker, something stronger
  Than love, patience, trust.

Enter an OLD WOMAN with a stick in her hand.

OLD WOMAN: Girl.
  You cry.
  Why?

FLORA: I…

OLD WOMAN: Yes?

FLORA: My husband…

OLD WOMAN: Ah!

FLORA: He's a pig.

OLD WOMAN: Most husbands are.
  When you've reached my age you'll know.
  There's no need to take on so.

FLORA: No.

He's a very nice pig.

A lovely pig.

But he's even lovelier when he's a man.

He's a pig in the day,

A man at night.

He's under a spell.

OLD WOMAN: Well, well.

Spells are everywhere these days.

It's spell this, spell that.

But spells can be broken. There's always ways.

Dry your eyes.

Let's have a little chat.

So, your husband's a pig.

It's happened before. It's not that big.

I can help you, dear.

Don't cry.

FLORA: Help me?

You want to help me?

Why?

OLD WOMAN: I'm a mother.

My daughter, like you,

Loved a man too,

But he turned out a proper pig.

He broke her heart.

Now, this spell –

Man to pig;

Pig to man.

If anyone can break that spell

I can.

FLORA: You can?

He'll be a man?

Tell. Tell.

Help me break the spell.

OLD WOMAN: (*Taking from her pocket a long thin red thread.*)
    See this thread,
    Thin and red.
    This thread is a magic thread.
    While he sleeps in human form
    Just before the crack of dawn
    Take this red and magic thread
    And tie his ankle to the bed.
    When he opens sleepy eyes
    As a man he will arise.
    The spell will be broken.

FLORA: (*Taking the thread.*)
    Magic thread
    Ties foot to bed.
    When he wakes
    The spell breaks.
    Thank you.

OLD WOMAN: No need for thanks.
    Oh, one other thing.
    About the string –
    He must not know.
    If he knows, the spell won't break.

FLORA: No. Not a word.
    Thank you.

OLD WOMAN: I do this for my daughter's sake.

FLORA: Night, come quickly as you can
    Bring my husband as a man.
    Sun, when next you rise, you'll see
    A man, my husband, next to me.
    Thank you. Thank you.

OLD WOMAN: To get what's hers
　　What won't a woman do?
　　A pig.

CHORUS: Slow day creeps.
　　Slow night falls.
　　Slow pig man.
　　Slow he sleeps.
　　Quick she leaps.
　　Quiet she crawls.
　　Quick spell break.
　　If thread can.

Night. PIG in bed asleep.

FLORA at the foot of the bed.

FLORA: Sleep, Husband, sleep.
　　When you wake
　　The spell will break.
　　I will restore your human form to you.
　　Wind, red thread, bind.
　　Wake to find
　　The dawn has torn
　　All that's of the pig from you.
　　Magic thread.
　　Foot to bed.
　　When he wakes
　　The spell...

PIG wakes up. The thread snaps.

PIG: Woman! What have you done?

FLORA: I have broken the spell.

PIG: No.

FLORA: But...

PIG: What you've broken is Love.
    What you've broken is Trust.

FLORA: But the Old Woman…she…

OLD WOMAN: (*Appearing and seizing PIG.*)
    Now you're mine!

PIG: This Old Woman is the witch who enchanted me.

OLD WOMAN: Now you must part for ever.

PIG: If you had loved me for three more nights
    Then her spell would have broken.
    True Love is stronger than any spell.

OLD WOMAN: You stupid Pig, you thought this girl could
    save you?

PIG: Three more nights…

OLD WOMAN: Her weak love?

PIG: Just three more nights…

OLD WOMAN: Her feeble trust?

PIG: And the spell would have broken.

FLORA: I was only trying…

PIG: Your love was not strong enough to save me.

OLD WOMAN: Now you must marry my daughter.

PIG: No love is.

OLD WOMAN: Her love is strong.

PIG: No love is.

OLD WOMAN: It will never let you go.
    (*To FLORA.*) You will never see him again.

PIG: We will never meet again.

OLD WOMAN: Not if you wore out three pairs of iron
shoes looking for him.
Come on, Pig. My daughter's waiting.

FLORA: Never? No! Don't say never. You must be wrong.

PIG: Wear out three pairs of iron shoes and search the
world for me,
Then I'll be free.
When shoes of iron, worn right through, drop from
your feet,
Then we'll meet.
But this, Love and you
Can never do.

PIG vanishes.

FLORA: It can.
I will.
Husband.
Love.
Fate.
Husband.
Love.
Wait.

End of Act Three.

Act Four

CHORUS: Wear out three pairs of iron shoes and search
    the world for me.
    Then I'll be free.
    When shoes of iron, worn right through, drop from
    your feet,
    Then we'll meet.
    Cold like the moon were metals that made them,
    Fierce as the sun were the hammers that beat
    The hard staff of steel that she bears in her hand,
    The harsh shoes of iron she wears on her feet.

PRINCESS: Iron-staffed,
    Iron-shod,
    Which road is
    The road Love trod?

CHORUS: On, Princess, on,
    Till three pairs of shoes are gone.
    Distance and geography
    Fail beneath your feet.
    Welded to your iron shoes,
    Pole and Tropic meet.

PRINCESS: Hope my compass.
    Love my star.
    Feet don't feel
    How tired you are.

CHORUS: On, Princess, on,
    Half an inch of iron gone.
    Stars and constellations
    Track you from above.
    Longitude and latitude
    Will never confound Love.

PRINCESS: Iron-staffed.
    Iron-shod.
    Hope my lantern.
    Love my God.

CHORUS: Through deserts and past glaciers
    She treads the planet's girth.
    Iron-staffed and iron-shod
    She walks right round the Earth.

PRINCESS: Sure of purpose.
    Love is true.
    I'm strong, Husband.
    I'll find you.

CHORUS: On, Princess, on.
    Look those shoes are nearly gone.

PRINCESS: Shoes wear thin,
    Staff starts to bend.
    I have walked
    To the World's End.

CHORUS: The World's End.
    A lonely place.
    Stone. Rock. Space.
    Ice and night.
    But there a light!
    And there – a name ! A door!
    Among the rocks.
    She reads.

PRINCESS: The North Wind.

CHORUS: She knocks.

Inside the house of the NORTH WIND.

NORTH WIND in an armchair.

MRS NORTH WIND making their tea.

NORTH WIND: Door! Woman! Door! You deaf or what?

MRS NORTH WIND: You answer it

NORTH WIND: I will not.
I'm tired out.

MRS NORTH WIND: I don't know how. You don't do nowt
All day but blow about
A bit.

More knocking.

NORTH WIND: That's it. Will you get that bleeding door.

MRS NORTH WIND: I can't take this anymore.
You idle sod.

NORTH WIND: Blow about a bit!
My God!
Get that door or I'll show you blowing.

MRS NORTH WIND: All right, you lazy get, I'm going.

NORTH WIND: Banging on the door this time of night.

MRS NORTH WIND opens the door.

There stands FLORA.

FLORA: I'm cold. I'm hungry. I saw your light.

MRS NORTH WIND: (*Bringing FLORA in.*)
Poor little pretty freezing thing.
Come in, my little duck, come in.

NORTH WIND: Who is it?

MRS NORTH WIND: How the beggar should I know?
You bleeding stupid so-and-so.
We'll soon have you warmed up; get you something to eat.

NORTH WIND: Tell her to wipe her feet.

MRS NORTH WIND: Don't mind him. He's the bane of my
    life.
    He's the North Wind. And me, for my sins, I'm his wife.

*As FLORA wipes her feet the iron shoes break and fall off
her feet.*

FLORA: Oh!
    These iron shoes have worn right through.
    I'm almost there.
    Just another two.
    I'll put on another pair.

She starts to put on a second pair of shoes.

NORTH WIND: Interesting footwear
    You've got there.

FLORA: I've lost my husband
    I must walk and walk
    And search for him
    Till I've worn out
    The iron shoes.

NORTH WIND: You could make quite a bruise
    With a well-aimed kick from an iron shoe.

MRS NORTH WIND: Lost your husband. Lucky you.

FLORA: You haven't seen him, have you?

MRS NORTH WIND: Who, dear?

NORTH WIND: Who?

FLORA: My husband.

MRS NORTH WIND: Of course, your husband.
    I was miles away.

NORTH WIND: I should be so lucky.

MRS NORTH WIND: Well, you spend all day
   Blowing about.
   Have you seen him?
   Help the girl out.

NORTH WIND: What, me? No.

MRS NORTH WIND: Typical. He's a useless so-and-so.

NORTH WIND: Well, you're no better, you don't know.

MRS NORTH WIND: Oh flaming Henry, here we go.
   Why don't you give that a rest.

NORTH WIND: A rest, I'd love a rest. From you.

MRS NORTH WIND: Well, you know what you can do.
   Thick-head.

NORTH WIND: Drop dead.

FLORA: Excuse me.

MRS NORTH WIND: Yes, my little chick, what is it?

FLORA: I hope that you don't think I'm rude.

MRS NORTH WIND: Rude, dear, rude?
   You're in the house of Mr Crude.

FLORA: I thought marriage was sweet, tender but strong.

NORTH WIND: I take it you weren't married long.

FLORA: The way you shout.
   The way you swear.
   Is this what couples have to bear?
   Is there any love left there?

NORTH WIND: Me love her?

MRS NORTH WIND: Me love him?

NORTH WIND: I love the bones of her.

MRS NORTH WIND: Every hair on his bleeding head.

NORTH WIND / MRS NORTH WIND: I love the curlers in
    her hair.
  I love his filthy underwear.
  I love the way he never knows
  When he's got bogies up his nose.
  I love the way her false teeth clack.
  I love his really hairy back.
  I love it when my programme starts,
  She sits in that armchair and farts.
  Oh we're in love all right, don't doubt it.
  We just don't make a song and dance about it.
  He'll blow his nose and have a look.
  I love the way that she can't cook.
  I love it when he isn't there.
  The plughole blocked with her grey hair.
  And just when I've abandoned hope,
  I find some more hair in the soap.
  The way he'll sit in that armchair
  And scratch his bum without a care.
  Oh we're in love all right, don't doubt it.
  We just don't make a song and dance about it.

NORTH WIND: I've just had a thought.

MRS NORTH WIND: Wonders will never cease.

NORTH WIND: The Moon.
  The Moon will know where your husband is.
  All he does is stand and stare
  At the world and the people there.
  Through the night he will have seen
  Where your husband is or where he's been.

FLORA: The Moon.

NORTH WIND: Well, come on, you stupid mare,
    Get my hat and my coat.
    I'm taking her there.

MRS NORTH WIND: Get them yourself, I'm not your slave.

NORTH WIND: Oh behave.

He goes to get his hat and coat.

MRS NORTH WIND unpins a jewel and gives it to FLORA.

MRS NORTH WIND: Here, dear, take this for luck.
    Keep it and don't forget
    We shout and scream.
    Kick up a stink,
    But Love is more mysterious than you'd think.

NORTH WIND: (*To FLORA.*)
    Ready? Come on then. Hold on tight.
    (*To MRS NORTH WIND.*) Get the bed warm. I'll be back
        tonight.

In the sky.

CHORUS: Wind and Princess hurtle through the night sky.
    Snow geese sing as they fly by.

SNOW GEESE: Cold he sleeps
    And cold he wakes
    And cold the hand
    That makes
    His bed.
    Cold his laughter.
    Cold his sighs
    And cold the breast
    Where lies
    His head.

In the night sky a bed with PIG on it.

On either side of him the OLD WOMAN and ADELAIDE.

FLORA: Husband! Love!

PIG: Princess! Love!

ADELAIDE: It's me he's going to marry, her he dreams
about.

OLD WOMAN: Calm, daughter, calm. Here is the drug that
snuffs memory out.

*The OLD WOMAN lifts a cup and pours the contents down
the PIG's throat.*

ADELAIDE: What about her, mother? The other?

OLD WOMAN: Don't you worry about the other. She won't
get through one shoe, let alone three.
Then he will love you, daughter. Trust me.

PIG: Princess! Wife!

ADELAIDE: Yes, dear, I'm here.

OLD WOMAN, PIG, ADELAIDE and the bed vanish.

NORTH WIND: My dear.
We're here.
In the palace of the Moon.

FLORA: Moon.

MOON: Sssh.
See. They see me.
I'm seen.
Silver. Serene.
Lovers, mariners
Look up and adore.
Reflected in their eyes
I set. I rise.
I wax. I wane.

I change. I'm the same.
What else should Love be?
They love me.
I love them so much
And we never touch.

FLORA: I wonder…

MOON: I know what you wonder.
I've seen you wonder
As you gaze up at me.
You want someone to touch.
Someone to know.
Intimacy.
Just let it be.
Love is mystery.

FLORA: I must find my husband.

MOON: Whatever you look at
It's him you see.
I look in your eyes
And it's his reflection.
Such constancy,
Such affection
Move me.
I haven't seen him.
The Sun will know.
He pays attention.
I'll take you.

He unpins a jewel and gives it to FLORA.

Have this.
Sometimes cloudy
Sometimes clear
Sometimes distant
Sometimes near.

A changeable jewel.
Like me.
Like love.
Keep it. Remember
Love is stranger than you know.
Let's go.

In the sky…

CHORUS: Moon and Princess sail through the pale night sky.
Clouds sing as they scud by.

CLOUDS: Cold he sits
And cold he stands
And cold the hands
That hold
His hand.
Cold the song
They coldly sing.
Cold the finger.
Cold the ring.

In the night sky a sofa with PIG propped up between ADELAIDE and the OLD WOMAN.

ADELAIDE flicking through wedding magazines.

FLORA: Husband!
Love!

PIG: Princess!
Wife!

ADELAIDE: Yes, I'm your little princess.
And soon I'll be your wife.
I go all tingly when I think
Soon you'll be mine
For life.
Mother, more drug, mother.

OLD WOMAN pours the drug down PIG's throat.

PIG: Princess! Wife!

ADELAIDE: I'm having that tiara
Those earrings and that brooch.
We're leaving the reception
In a glass pumpkin-shaped coach.
More drug, mother, quick, mother.

OLD WOMAN pours more drug down PIG's throat.

PIG: Princess! Wife!

ADELAIDE: Wait till you see the flowers.
Wait till you see the ring.

OLD WOMAN: Isn't love a beautiful thing?

They vanish.

PRINCESS: Love!
Love!
Gone!

MOON: Our journey's done.
We've reached the sun.
And that's Day,
His fiancée.

*The SUN's palace. Gaudy. A jacuzzi. DAY, tanned and in
Gucci, runs in screaming.*

DAY: Aaaaaaaaah!

The SUN, tanned and muscled, comes flying in after her.

SUN: Come here! Come here you!

DAY: Oooooh
What you going to do?

SUN: Come here and see.

DAY: Not me.

SUN: I'm going to get you.

DAY: Says who?

SUN: Says me.

DAY: Eeeeeeeeeeee!

The SUN catches DAY and snogs her.

SUN: Come on, let's play.

DAY: What?

SUN: Hide-and-seek.

DAY: What like before?
   You always hide behind the door.

SUN: Chase the Lady.
   Blindman's Buff.

DAY: We've played Blindman's Buff enough.

SUN: Hunt the Slipper.
   Pillow-fight.
   Will you?
   Won't you?

DAY: Well, I might.

SUN: Sardines.

DAY: Doctors.

SUN: Peekaboo.
   I just want to play with you.

DAY: Oooooooh!

FLORA: Hello.

SUN: (*Without looking at FLORA.*)
  Hello.
  Let's go and play. Where would be best?

DAY: Don't forget. We've a guest. We haven't met. This is
  the Sun.

SUN: Hi. Let's get away

DAY: I'm Day, his fiancée.
  What can we do for you today?
  (*She scans FLORA.*)
  Oooooh
  Nice shoes.
  In a way.
  They suit you
  But they're worn away.

FLORA: They wore through
  With the Moon.
  That's two.
  I find him soon.
  Another pair
  And I'll be there.

She takes off the worn-out shoes and puts the last pair on.

DAY: Find who?

SUN: Be where?

FLORA: My husband.
  I've been searching everywhere.
  I've worn out two pairs of iron shoes.
  I must find him soon. There's no time to lose.

DAY: That's so romantic.
  If I lost you, babe, I'd be frantic.
  I'd even wear an iron shoe
  For you.

SUN: I love you.

DAY: I love you too.

FLORA: I don't know what to do.
    I walked around the world,
    Halfway across the sky.
    I'll never find him.

SUN: Here, your husband?

FLORA: Yes?

SUN: Quite a fit bloke?
    About this big?
    Used to be a pig?

FLORA: Yes.

SUN: Yeah I've seen him. The other day.

FLORA: You've seen him? Where?

SUN: Up the Milky Way.

FLORA: The Milky Way. I must get there.

DAY: It isn't that far.
    The Sun will take you there.

SUN: Oh, babe.

DAY: Yes, babe, you will. Don't make a fuss.
    Not everyone is lucky like us.

SUN: Selfless, that's you.

    He goes off to get ready.

    DAY unpins a jewel and gives it to FLORA.

DAY: Here take this. I've got loads of the stuff.
    Jewellery – he can't give me enough.
    You should look your best when you find him.

Good luck, girl. When you've found him, drop by for a
    drink.
Here's my darling.
Love's fantastic, don't you think?

SUN is ready.

SUN: Ready?

FLORA: Ready.

SUN: (*To DAY.*)
    Be ready.

DAY: I'm always ready.

SUN: Off we go.

DAY: Cheerio.
    In the sky.

CHORUS: Sun and Princess course through the sky
    Stars sing as they float by.

STARS: Cold his lips
    And cold his eyes.
    Warm him, Princess,
    Or he dies.
    Dead to you
    He'll ever be.
    Find him, warm him,
    Set him free.

SUN: It's the Milky Way.
    Can't stay. (*Exit.*)

FLORA: Now I'm going to find him.

THE MILKY WAY: Bright as Love.
    Strange as Love.
    Brittle as Love.

We glitter like Love.
Vast as Love.
Sharp as Love.
Hard as Love.
Climb us, your love
Sleeps above.

FLORA: Brittle stars scratch and tear.
Wear down my shoes, the final pair.
Stars, more white than my childhood's crown.
Iron shoes snap,
Tumble down
Soundless through space.
His face.

The last pair of shoes falls through space.

End of Act Four.

Act Five

SCENE 1

A hall in a palace at the top of the Milky Way. Enter FLORA.

FLORA: Love! Are you here?
Love, I have walked round the world for you.
Love, the iron has worn right through.
Love, I harnessed the Wind, Moon and Sun.
Love, what haven't I done?
Love, you are hard and bitter. See.
Love, what you have made me.

SLAVES enter frantically, some carry a massive wedding cake, others gaudy decorations and flowers. They consult lists and plans. They are very busy.

SLAVES: Wedding bell. Wedding vow.
The bride's just smashed the wedding cake. What's
wrong now?
She's getting married in three nights' time.

SLAVE 1: We need some more banners and bunting and stuff.
We need more confetti, there isn't enough.
If there's not there'll be hell to pay.

FLORA: Excuse me…

SLAVE 1: Get out of the way.

SLAVE 2: Are you sure that the quail in the quail vol-au-vents
Is the same sort of quail as the quail that she wants?
If it's not there'll be hell to pay.

FLORA: Excuse me.

SLAVE 2: Get out of the way.

SLAVE 3: The seating plan's full up with guests of the bride,
But no one's been asked to come from the groom's side.
It's going to be hell on the day.

FLORA: Excuse me.

SLAVES: Will you get out of the way.
Wedding vow. Wedding bell.
It's got to be all perfect or she'll make life hell.
She's getting married in three nights' time.

A tiara hurtles across the stage.

Enter ADELAIDE, furious.

ADELAIDE: Tiara!
Do you call this a tiara?
I want a proper tiara!
Not this thing!
I had more sparkle from beads on an old bit of string!
I want shine!
I want bling!
And the veil?
Where's the veil?

SLAVE 4: The design was so fine that four of the nuns who
were making it found they'd gone blind.

ADELAIDE: Do I look like I mind
If some nuns have gone blind?
The whole bleeding convent can drop down dead
Just so long as that veil is on top of my head
By tonight.
All right?
And the swan?
Where's it gone?
The sixteen-foot swan
That I'm sitting on
As I'm pulled up the aisle

By those dwarves.
God! Those dwarves!
Send them back!
I said all along
I want dwarves that are strong
And those dwarves can't lift up my train.
Send them all back again
And get out and hustle
Some midgets with muscle.
And the doves!
The doves that are being released
When I stand in front of the priest
And say 'I do' –
They won't do.
Shoot them all.
They're too small.
Maybe it's me
But I like a dove you can see.
Is it really too much to ask?
Have I set some impossible task?
I just want some sparkle.
I want things to shine.
It's my wedding.
Mine! Mine!
It's like some awful conspiracy.
Why can't you get it?
Why don't you see?
It's my wedding.
So who's it about?
It's my wedding.
I don't want to shout
But it's my wedding
So it's all about
ME!
Now get out! And don't come back till everything's
    perfect.

Exit SLAVES. ADELAIDE spots FLORA.

ADELAIDE: Oi! You!
Haven't you got something to do?

ADELAIDE spots the jewel.

Oooh!
That jewel!
It's just what I've been looking for.
It would so go with my dress.

FLORA: Yes?
Here.
Look.
See it shine.

ADELAIDE: I wish it were mine.

FLORA: I'll lend it to you.

FLORA gives ADELAIDE the jewel.

ADELAIDE: Well, lend wasn't quite what I had in mind.

FLORA: Look at it shine.

ADELAIDE: How come a beautiful jewel is owned by a
grubby girl like you?

FLORA: The Wife of the North Wind gave it to me.
She said Love was more mysterious than I knew.

ADELAIDE: Mysterious?
More like painful.
Agonising.
But then,
What would a girl like you
Know of love,
Know of men?

FLORA: Nothing.
  I know nothing about love.
  Tell me.

ADELAIDE: My husband to be –
  Of course he loves me,
  But sometimes he calls out –

FLORA: What?

ADELAIDE: Princess! Love!

FLORA: (*Aside.*)
  Husband! Love!
  I have found you at last!

ADELAIDE: In three nights' time
  I marry him. Then he will be mine.
  But till that night
  I will not let him out of my sight.
  But I must. I need my beauty sleep.
  I need someone who'll keep watch.
  I need a spy.

FLORA: Lady, I will be your spy.

ADELAIDE: You?

FLORA: Me.
  You can trust me.
  A grubby girl who knows nothing about Love or men.
  I will watch him.
  That jewel.
  Keep it. Look your best.
  I will watch him.
  You can rest.

ADELAIDE: All right.
  You can watch him tonight.
  Twinkle, jewel, shine.

Wearing this
He'll give me a kiss
For your sake
If not for mine.

FLORA: Everything's going to turn out all right.
Rise, Moon, and shine.
With a kiss
Spells
Will break
And you will be mine.

Exit ADELAIDE and FLORA.

SCENE 2

PIG's bedroom.

PIG: Sunset.
I seem to remember a feeling.
I seem to remember a face.
Was it love?
I forget.

Enter ADELAIDE with a cup.

ADELAIDE: Drink, my love, deep.
The sun has set.
Sleep, my love, sleep.
Sleep and forget.

PIG drinks and sleeps.

Enter FLORA.

He sleeps.

Keep watch. (*Exit.*)

FLORA: Wake up. It's me.
Wake up! I've come to set you free.

Wake up! Wake up! My love was strong.
Wake up! What's the matter with you?
Wake up! What's wrong?
North Wind, help me!
North Wind, howl!
Shake him!
Wake him!
Blow the sleep from his eyes.

NORTH WIND: A stronger power than my breath
Holds him in a living death.

FLORA: Day breaks.
He doesn't wake.

Enter ADELAIDE.

ADELAIDE: Well?

FLORA: Not a murmur,
Not a word.
How's your tiara?

ADELAIDE: Tiara?
Don't even mention tiara.
It's a tiara tragedy.
A tiara farce.
I'd like to shove that tiara right up her…

FLORA: Look. Would this help?
Take it. Wear it.
Look at it shine.

ADELAIDE: Look at it. Mine.
You'll watch again tonight?

FLORA: Yes, I'll watch again tonight.

ADELAIDE: Glitter, jewel, shine.
Two more nights
And he'll be mine.

SCENE 3

In the kitchen all the SLAVES are preparing for the wedding.

SLAVES: Wedding cake.
  Wedding bell.
  The bride is blooming
  But the groom's not well.
  He's getting married in two nights' time.

Enter the OLD WOMAN with some herbs and a cup.

OLD WOMAN: Here, you
  Grind these herbs up
  For my brew.
  Grind them finely,
  Grind them up.
  Pop them in the magic cup.
  This will put him fast asleep.
  What my daughter's got, she'll keep.

Enter ADELAIDE.

SLAVES: Wedding bell.
  Wedding cake.
  Somebody's making a terrible mistake.

OLD WOMAN: Here, dear, the drug is ready.
  Take up the cup.
  What's the matter?

ADELAIDE: Mother, why do you do what you do?

OLD WOMAN: Do you love him?

ADELAIDE: I love him.

OLD WOMAN: Then nothing's too much trouble for my
    special little girl.

ADELAIDE: You always say I'm special.

OLD WOMAN: You have an inner beauty.

ADELAIDE: The lengths you will go to.

OLD WOMAN: It's just a mother's duty.

ADELAIDE: The first time that I saw him.

OLD WOMAN: You saw him and you knew.

ADELAIDE: So you dragged him here and drugged him.

OLD WOMAN: It's what any mum would do.
Remember, dear, what's important here is your happiness.
No self-respecting mother would dream of doing less.
So be happy
Be happy
And don't get depressed.

ADELAIDE: I'll be happy.

OLD WOMAN: Be happy.

OLD WOMAN / ADELAIDE: Because mother knows best.

OLD WOMAN: Now you run along and drug your fiance.

Exit ADELAIDE.

Bless. (*Exit.*)

SCENE 4

PIG's bedroom.

PIG: Moonrise.
I seem to remember a voice
Calling to me from above.
Calling out:
Love!
I remember her eyes.

Enter ADELAIDE with the cup.

ADELAIDE: Sleep, love, forget.
Let sleep's tangled net

Enfold you.
Drink from the cup.
Drink it all up.
Let sleep and forgetfulness
Hold you.

PIG drinks and sleeps.

Enter FLORA. He sleeps.

Keep watch. (*Exit.*)

FLORA: Wake up! I've walked round the world to find you!
Wake up! Wake up! What can I do?
Help me, Moon, shine strong! Shine bright!
Help me break the spell tonight.

MOON: A stronger power than my beams
Keeps him wrapped in deadly dreams.

FLORA: Day has broken.
He hasn't woken.

Enter ADELAIDE.

ADELAIDE: Well?

FLORA: Not a murmur,
Not a word.
How's your dress?

ADELAIDE: Frankly a mess.
I think the front lacks focus.

FLORA: Would this help?
Take it. Wear it.
Look at it shine.

ADELAIDE: Look at it. Mine.
I'll look divine.
You'll watch tonight?
Just one more night.

FLORA: (*Giving the jewel.*)
   Just one more night.

ADELAIDE: Glitter, jewel, shine.
   One more night
   And he'll be mine.

SCENE 5

Kitchen. SLAVES getting ready for the wedding.

SLAVES: Wedding dress.
   Wedding veil.
   The bride looks happy
   But the groom's gone pale.
   He's getting married in one night's time

Enter FLORA.

SLAVE 1: Here, you, make yourself useful
   And grind these herbs up
   For the cup
   That the bride takes up
   Every night to the groom
   In his room.

FLORA: A cup to his room every night?

SLAVE 2: That's right. He needs to be drugged to marry a
      girl that rough.

FLORA: They drug him?

SLAVE 2: Yes.

SLAVE 3: That's enough.

SLAVE 2: Well, wouldn't you need to be off your head to
      wed a girl like the boss's daughter?

SLAVE 3: You've said more than you oughter.

FLORA: They drug him.
  Of course.
  Sun go down.
  Moon come up.
  Tonight you'll not drink from the cup.
  Tonight, my love, you'll wake for me.
  Tonight, my love, I'll set you free.

SLAVES: Wedding veil.
  Wedding dress.
  Somebody's in a terrible mess.

PIG: (*Offstage.*)
  Princess! Love! I remember…

FLORA: Everything's going to turn out all right.
  Husband! Love!

OLD WOMAN: (*Offstage.*)
  Grind those herbs up.
  Mother knows best.

ADELAIDE: Glitter, jewel, shine.
  One more night and he'll be mine.

SCENE 6

PIG's bedroom.

PIG: The sun sinks down,
  The moon comes up,
  I remember a girl with a crown.
  I remember her face.
  I remember another night.
  Another place.
  Not like this.
  I remember her kiss.
  Yes.
  I remember happiness.

Enter ADELAIDE with the cup.

ADELAIDE: Tomorrow we marry.
  Happy?

PIG: I'm close to happy
  I think.

ADELAIDE: Drink.

Enter FLORA. She throws the cup to the ground.

FLORA: No! Don't drink!
  It's drugged! She's poisoning you!

ADELAIDE: What the hell do you think you're doing,
  You grubby little nobody?

FLORA: Get away from him.
  Get away from my husband.

ADELAIDE: Husband! So it's you!
  You're that princess.
  You're the other.
  Mother! Mother! (*Exit.*)

PIG: Princess, Love, Wife.

FLORA: Husband, Love, Life.

PIG: Love, Wife,
  Love, that walked the world.
  Love, stronger than iron,
  Love, that finds me, frees me, saves me.
  Love, stronger, stranger than I knew.
  Love. You.

FLORA: Husband.

PIG: Wife.

FLORA: Happy the princess whose crown breaks.
  Happy the woman Love blisters and blinds.

PIG: Happy the man that Love wakes
    And happy the fate that he finds.

OLD WOMAN / ADELAIDE: (*Entering suddenly.*)
    We've more spells, more drugs.
    You thought a pig was bad?
    A pig is luxury.
    This time you'll be a centipede!
    An earwig!
    And you, you cow, a cow.

PIG / FLORA: No charms can harm a love like ours.

OLD WOMAN: I have no powers.
    No magic art.

ADELAIDE: The spell is broken. So's my heart.

CHORUS: Look! A princess has found her fate.
    Her fate is Love. She thinks Love's great.
    Love makes you the hero. Love makes you a fool.
    Love makes you happy. Love makes you cruel.
    Love is a long and blood-red thread.
    Love is a battlefield. Love is a bed.
    Love is a wonder, more strange than you'd think.
    It's a drug. It's the dregs of a poisonous drink.
    Love gives you blisters. Love leaves you blind.
    Love is the rarest jewel you can find.
    Love leaves you crying. Love rocks you with laughter.
    Love lets you live happily ever after.
    Happy the princess whose crown breaks.
    Happy the woman Love blisters and blinds.
    Happy the man that Love wakes
    And happy the fate that he finds.

THE END